WHAT I STOLE

WHAT
I STOLE

DIANE SHER LUTOVICH

SIXTEEN RIVERS PRESS · SAN FRANCISCO

My thanks to the editors of the following publications, in which
these poems previously appeared:

Anemonie: "Objets d'Art"
Barnabe Mountain Review: "Intention," "Old Growth,"
    "In the Bridal Salon"
Footsteps: "At the State Theater on Saturday Afternoon"
Knowing Stones: Poems of Exotic Places: "Flesh and Spirit"
Lucid Stone: "Provenance"
Marin Arts Council: "Flowing," "In Egypt"
Medaphors: "Flowing"
Marin Poetry Center Anthology, Volume II: "Love and Syntax"
VIVO: "Silent Cities"
Wild Dove, Jane's Stories II: An Anthology by Midwestern Women:
    "Nosound"

Cover art: *Seated Figure with Hat,* by Richard Diebenkorn, oil on
canvas, reprinted with permission of The National Gallery of Art,
Washington, D.C.

Cover/book design: Christi Payne, Book Arts

Published by Sixteen Rivers Press
P.O. Box 640663
San Francisco, CA 94164-0663
www.sixteenrivers.com

ISBN 0-9707370-5-X
Library of Congress Catalog Card Number: 2002-036580

For those who want to keep the past present

In this world, there are two times. There is mechanical time and there is body time. The first is as rigid and metallic as a massive pendulum of iron that swings back and forth. . . . The second squirms and wriggles like a bluefish in a bay. The first is unyielding, predetermined. The second makes up its mind as it goes along.

—ALAN LIGHTMAN, *EINSTEIN'S DREAMS*

CONTENTS

What Remains

THE
THINGS
WE
WORSHIP

Donaciana Aquiree Gives Thanks

*The words are smudged, my Spanish poor, but I
know this: Donaciana Aquiree commissioned
this retablo on the occasion of giving thanks for
(it gets vague) her husband (a su esposo), but
for what? (the words disappear)*

She is kneeling, pitched precariously
in her black cloak, eyes turned in and up
toward God and her saint

the only uncovered flesh—a speck of face,
fingers clutching her robe

Her saint smiles wanly, his little foot
creeps out from his cloak
as if to have congress with her hand

he holds two fingers out to God;
in his other hand, the world rests

He, righteous, impassive; she, so grateful, so small

But for what miracle
did she pay some itinerant painter
to paint her thanks on a scrap of tin, shard of oil can
in Pátzcuaro, in 1907?

Did God cure her *esposo* or take him?
Did her man stop drinking, get a job,
stop being or become impotent?

Something happened

big enough for Donaciana to spend her savings
on this image of her gratitude,
which hangs,

her gratitude hangs

her faith hangs

on a California wall

a testimonial to
prayers answered.

In Certain Light

Rothko's painting changes,
background slips into foreground,
red canvas to gray stripe
scratched through the center
homage to slipperiness,
sensual longing of contrasts.

Tongue starts feeling ripe,
hungry for something.

The way I crave a hand in mine
or flesh against my flesh
never forgetting

that afternoon on the deck of our room
Lake Palace Hotel, Udaipur,
ancient Indian sun melting each fold, sweat pooling
into each dip of flesh.
Slowly, pants off, then shirts.
Two bodies stopped
to rest, floated
upward and down,
to discover temples
in the precise blurring of background, foreground.

All Is Gold

When runners carrying gold to free
their king, Atahualpa, heard he'd been
strangled, they buried the gold beneath
their feet.
—JOHN HEMMING, THE CONQUEST OF THE INCAS

Paddling this astonishing
Pacific-bound stream, I'm caught
by the sun shedding,
sprinkling golden discs
merging, separating,
finally binding themselves
into one blinding path
leading up and back.

No wonder Egyptians, Incas,
all people living close
to the world, craved gold
as if cast off by the sun,
one blaze illuminating the wearer,
mirroring its source. In death
they covered themselves with
the same sacred sun-reflecting surface.

This morning I could have
paddled or drowned in that path
dragged across the water by the sun
trolling for people like me
who want to melt into its power,
but are too frightened
to approach its center, afraid
of burning their eyes,
never finding home again.

It Was the Venetians Who Knew Light

how it floats up from lagoon depths,
bounces through clouds,
falls back to earth more washed and holy.

Sun but a tool for dispensing,
gathering light from deep inside,

the way Tiepolo sucked that pale washed light
out of the eighteenth century
imprinted it on virgins at annunciations, presentations,
always at assumptions.

How some mornings light spreads
from a speck of ash
to a miracle of faith, glazing cathedrals,
lagoons, stooped black-clad women
in a glow

so pure that holding your hand
up to the sky
you see nothing but light
broken here and there by a few
blue veins,

vague outline of bone, blot of muscle,
as if we were more and more light,
less and less structure.

Sacred Images

If I were Hiroshige,
awl and wood block at hand,
I'd spend hours memorizing
the egret's neck,
marking its expanding, contracting

across a slender
inlet meandering
into the greater Pacific.

But then I'd turn inward,
carve each bamboo branch,
fishing boat with its flapping sails,
fish (no bigger than an eyelash)
dangling from rods,
solitary fishing village,
people too small for features
scurrying home to dinner.

Flesh and Spirit

Mogul invaders called the carvings
satanic. The British called them "love temples,"
kept their ladies away.

But it's not their humping and thumping,
riding and sucking that makes me
want to rip off my clothes,
dive into a warm-fleshed man

                   but that they're having such fun.

Erotic is not about
position,
it's about pleasure

about the way she fondles his eyes
with her eyes, her mouth
ripening into a half smile,
the way he holds her breast like a golden bird.

Looking at hundreds of bodies
carved from one piece of stone,
joined without friction,

                  easy enough to worship the universe
                  in the midst of bodies,
                  curling like vines,
                  around, into each other.

Easy enough to wear the inside of your body
outside—relive all moments when
flesh and spirit join,

like flying off the high board, the body
slicing the water in two.

Wondering About Water, Forgetting About Time

1.
Yesterday at low tide, silt
shut the slough like a trap,
mud stranded boats on docks
perched high above water.

Birds hid,
everything waited
for solace
or a recognition of
some huge error.

2.
Today I want to rejoice
in the day's fullness—
overflow of water
birds calling to food,
sun richer by reflection.

Instead I study tide tables
like obituaries,
know about deposits of silt,
quickening of tides,
future dovetailing the past
in ways I don't like.

3.
Tonight a full moon—
I try to expand to its promise
to the way it graces the moment

but what I see is water
starting to shrink,
moon starting to slide.

So Much Depends

Across the creek
a yellow canoe so bright, so lurid,
color hangs suspended
between dock and sky—

a yellow screaming from the planet's
other side, jags
like a spark, frequency,
small explosion, and yet

or maybe, therefore
it lights up
a gray day sending air
leaping;
its reflection
burnishes the creek's
dead water.

On a gray day, as the year
winds down
with all earth's early promises
smashed to smithereens,
that color, phony as it is,
beckons, like hope.
This year, that must do.

The Giraffe

Watch how it lopes,
barely connected kite-
like across the savannah,
neck parting air
with its longing.

Sky forms it,
wraps it in clouds.
When sun disappears, it melts
into soft winds fleecing
moisture from leaves.

Forcing us always to remember—
so much bone and cartilage
moving relentlessly, surviving—
a testimony to Darwin or Lamarck or
hope—sharing secrets
with hunters and the hunted.

Needing earth, it is more air,
pulls air from the story
of its life.

Each step denies and verifies
how survival requires
more—the need to stretch

between where our feet take us,
what our heads can almost imagine.

Name/Be Named

Say   *snake*

                    Hear the transparent
                      sloughed-off skin.

                           See its supple cunning
                      slither vertically, teasing air.
                    Its coral tongue
                  leaps—sounds

in the circumference of its mouth—

                  Between unhinged jaws,   all words
                      fall
                        from our dreams,
            weave us into   sounds.

                       Skin
                           touching
                               words
                        whimpered
                    hope breathed deeply.

          All that lurks

in the back of dreams, in the front

   of all charmers' baskets
coiled deeply, waiting.

Nosound

Sunday afternoons on Elm Avenue, nosound
throbs. Once it was the nosound of a Minnesota afternoon
on the eve of VJ Day. Air wrapped trees,
stifled birds; summer heat stuck to cement, between
fingers. On Sixth Avenue, only ghosts of cars moved;
real ones, stripped of rubber and oil,
rested on blocks.

In those days, I moved through space
as if it were cream; my father could vaporize,
the spaniel rolled its whimpers
into black fur,
we heard the sun set.

Now, when nosound shrouds my street
where cats usually caterwaul and cars and dogs groan,

my skin tightens,
hands become ears.

It is the nosound of my daughter's room,
abandoned on her way to life, leaving
outgrown socks,
unmatched shoes.

Of the moments after the dead are covered with dirt
and mourners have returned to their homes,

the nosound of blackberries thickening
on my father's grave.

It is the nosound of an empty sky after
green and gold shards, left by the last fireworks,
have turned into stars.

LOVE
AND
SYNTAX

Die knowing something.
You are not here long.
—WALKER EVANS

Beginnings

The last time I heard "Tigris and Euphrates"
Miss Gandsey unrolled the map
as if the world had turned away
for blackboard and chalk

pointed to the place between thin blue lines
the place where the world began

the Fertile Crescent

the oasis near Genesis

first man, woman

on the first day of high school

Northern Minnesota off the frame
    infertile, except for deep veins
      of iron

and our newly fertile selves
wondering, in straight rows,
air, dry and cold,
about beginnings
ours at fourteen, hot-breathed
in hard seats
straining to see the thin blue lines
of rivers
thinner than wrist veins
boundaries of the fertile crescent
last known home of Adam and Eve
before they were banished
from green moss and warmth.

Provenance

In the dining room, the collage of a Chilean woman,
bought years ago, falls away;
her chest, almost bare of tissue strips and cloth,
her face frees colored bits of paper and newsprint. Each day
she's less collage,
more primal canvas.

On my face, patches of other-colored skin;
two deep brown patches punctuate
each cheekbone, the work, they say, of time and sun.

But suppose time and sun do not discolor,
simply wear through the thin veneer of pale skin
formed before birth to blend us into this life,
patina wearing away, revealing Navaho or Cree skin,
or Semitic skin of a desert nomad.

They shouldn't be removed, these signs of transition,
becoming or uncoming, exposing;
like love, the way scattered patches of hunger
for holding and stretching erupt
through toughened, self-contained flesh
revealing desire or whatever
waits underneath.

Love and Syntax

Before I met him, I spoke
in the subjunctive; men
found my fear, lack of trust,
mildly erotic—a Girl Scout turned inside
out, stripped naked.

Subjective was the road
in and out of the terror
in the back of my throat.

We were driving down the coast
after our first weekend together,
Pacific on our right,
grazing sheep between
us and the horizon—
almost biblical when he answered

my conditional
with a declarative
turning around the very syntax
of my dreams—"if" and "when" emptied
like contents of pill bottles, leaving
only echoes of breathless,
fearful consonants.

To my "If we . . . "
he replied, "Let's just
say this is the way . . . "

Forcing me into the
interrogative, another form
of love talk—
fearful, dependent questions . . . "Well do you . . . "
and he passed the blue
Volvo ahead.
About that moment I felt
some tectonic plate shift,
my language became unrecognizable—
words that covered my ears, tongue,
were altered.

Over these years I've learned to use
not only declaratives but exclamations,
commands. When our bodies
join I hear myself murmuring
"I want"
again and again
until   only silence.

Objets d'Art

Gauguin's women, draped like hibiscus,
add color to the porch. Curved hips,
shoulders break straight edge
of porch, horizon, repeat
arch of the breeze, sun's heat.
The arrangement reflects his commands:
"You with the blue shirt,
lean on your right hand.
You in the red dress sprawl
on your belly, lift
your chin."

When he took them in bed, he arranged
their folds: "You with the sharp nipples,
place a pillow under your hips, hands behind your neck."

And like a bowl of purple grapes
or golden peaches
they remained
part of his still-life.

Each one, later burning
with syphilis,
said she saw in his eyes the imprint
of her soul.

Do Not Answer the Phone

It will ring on October 17, 1963, at 7 P.M.
It will ring several times.
You will be tempted. Turn on
the shower or vacuum; take a walk.
If you pick it up, say she's not home;
she joined the Peace Corps, a convent,
is waiting trial for murder. If you answer
and reveal your name, say no, say it many times,
say it loud enough to drown out the invitations to sail,
to hear Leontyne Price sing *La Forza del Destino.*
If you accept, turn your cheek to the kiss, withdraw your hand
into your pocket, say you have no free time
for 1,248 days, say you are frigid, you have to get home;
your mother calls at 11:30.

You'll ignore this warning.
You'll learn to convince yourself
you always wanted to separate
your heart from your body; that joy
melts on the back of the tongue.
And I promise nearly four decades later
you'll still wear regret, see
pale scars, a mouth frozen this side of a smile.

It Was a Launching of Sorts

On her way to die she announced "It's been a good life, I'm ready." We met over Yeats—he was reading "Sailing to Byzantium." I wanted his hand immediately. On our way over the bridge, contractions increased and we could see the Farallons. I had packed a tie-dyed blanket to wrap her in. She said, "I'm ready," I called the family. Her breaths, still steady, slowed. He talked of his boys and his love of Brahms, his finely turned ear which my tongue kept reaching for along with French horns. She kept saying I'm ready while I rubbed her feet trying to hold her here a little longer. I wasn't ready to stop forming the word for *mother*. The contractions quickened—a crowning, a calm. I wanted to go home. He said he'd call and I was ready; I had waited forever to use *love* as a noun. Our fingers curled around each others'. Nurses removed the IV to speed her departure, they said; no one mentioned *dead* or *dying*—her white face, white hair, white sheet, gurgling of old air escaping from exhausted lungs. Contractions started again. I was ready and pushed as ordered and she came flying out. He recited "The Palm at the End of the Mind." Her heart finally stopped; she deflated into an old reflection or memory. We ordered a coffin. They swaddled the newborn, laid her on my belly. He sent me a dozen roses. With all its physical and linguistic adaptations I entered into a new life.

Old Growth

I refuse to notice the commode in the middle of his room,
wheelchair he's strapped to,
to remember our first night
how he peeled back my clothes and, without knowing me,
used those long, tapered pianist's fingers to explore,
discard all but what he needed.

I try to focus on those lifeless fingers
splayed across the table,
tough, thick nails he asks me to clip.

We both understand that lust, satisfied,
leaves in its wake goodwill, mutual obligation.
So I take each hand, helpless as a sleeping baby,
newborn kitten, into my lap,
line up the nails and clippers—a surgical nurse
trained to snip body parts,
tree surgeon, to snip branches of elm.

He warns me that clipped skin of paralyzed fingers
feels pain. I squeeze the clippers with both hands;
we watch those pieces of vestigial armor snap off,
careen beyond the wastebasket.

I refuse to look in his eyes, though our heads
bob, inches apart, as if we're examining some treasure.

What the Body Knows

Hiking up the canyon
in the Prima Vera Wilderness,
feet balance, thighs thrust,
the body a part of and separate from

My mind wanders
to lunch, last evening's talk,
my eyes register hunks of worked obsidian,
blistering blue lady slippers, *violeta de monte*

I leave feet struggling for foothold
to make their way without
guidance—resting on plateaus, digging into
slippery scree, stepping away from
treacherous spikes of *agave tequilana*

Salty sweat slides down cheeks,
into creases of elbows, that fine crevasse
between thigh and pelvis, under breasts,
leaving me moist with exertion

Spiraling back to base,
I think of these body parts
turning in love, how here, too,
head sneaks off to its own vistas,
memories, caches of desire
drawing from me the wonder
of joining and unfolding

as if we started a hike up the arroyo together
and returned damp, joyous, sated.

An Authentic Existence

*The individual must find his spiritual path, not
through the comfortable dogmatic rituals of the
established church, but through action, action
that is conscious of religious conviction.*
—SØREN KIERKEGAARD, FEAR AND TREMBLING

They move around
over my head on the third floor
she with the blank eyes
endlessly asking; he, contemplating
his life work—Kierkegaard, who had nothing
to say about loving a wife
who disappeared leaving
only her body behind.

He wheels her out to his car,
lifts her in, not a burden
but a wife he vowed, six, seven decades ago
to lift. His gray eyes still bloom and I wonder
in the midst of his mercy
if I couldn't
creep up the stairs
knock softly on his door and take
his elderly, naked body into my own
so all mercy is not hoarded.

It would be my religious
conviction, an action removed
of dogmatic rituals, the only
faith I know.

Once she asked him
"what" twelve times. Each time he answered,
a voice detached from its own pain,
disembodied—over and over
"Betty, it's nothing. You can sleep now."

It Sang: I Cried

AFTERNOON

Sailing the bay
swells tipping us
side to side

Typical

but for misplaced cormorants
circling mid-bay, careening into white caps
haunting the surface

Suddenly

through golden mists
spray erupts
a whale rises up
flaunts its back
flukes roiling
churning water

I hear myself cry out from
some buried place

Then it breaches again
And I cry again

When the whale disappears for good
slick water holds its shadow

NIGHT

I want to embrace
a body,
as if the skin's fullness,
tenderness,
would reinforce the joy, surprise,
keep open those closed places

that forget what remains
when you think
it's all run out.

They Never Told Us

light slices through regret,
burnishes old candlesticks,
makes a jewel of the blue vein
quivering in the throat's center.

As my daughter, her father, and I
sit around the table, guests gone,
cake shedding its last crumbs,
fruit salad blackening around the edges,
we talk of things—
NAFTA, NOW, postmodern art.

Joy rises into the throat,
pressing against that small place,
vulnerable as eggshell or bone china,
so easy to smash.

This, for the moment, perfect creature,
reminder of love's failure and success,
sits and talks—even
as her new sophisticated hairstyle wilts into the late
December afternoon, the dimming light
forms concentric circles—
we sit, afraid to break the moment.

Not easy to find that place called love—

but in the deepening reflection on the polished table, it gets close
to cutting itself loose as a word
and becoming.

WHAT
I
STOLE

What I Stole

I stole endlessly
as if the center of the universe
were all mine.

I stole brazenly,
stripped off my clothes to steal gazes,
entire pages from the encyclopedia,
attention and time from teachers,
glances from mirrors.

I stole others' ideas,
my father's succulence,
Snickers bars from the five-and-dime,
a seat in the Sweet Shoppe,
pencils from other students—
one stamped "Thou shalt not steal"—
my best friend's lover (I did give him back).

I stole change from vending machines,
books from libraries,
heat from the homeless,
affections of careless but devoted men,
lines from Garbo, Dietrich,
dreams from Jung,
my mother's dreams of a faultless daughter,
my daughter's dreams of a faultless mother,

sunfish mired in the sandy bottom of Beatrice Lake,
seedlings from roadside plants,
lilacs from strangers' bushes.

I stole stars from winter skies,
the moon's light to read by.
Even my life, so full of sweet apricots, scent of jasmine,
babies' laughter, must have belonged to someone else.

Gifts from the Dead

The Christmas cactus I stole
from your porch after
they took you away to die
still blazes almost thirty years later.

Engorged tips of wandering
limbs, hot fuschia-hued
blossoms shroud
pistils and stamens.

Petals pale, drop; daily I retrieve them
shriveled like the umbilical cords
the mama cat chewed off,
dropped around my bedroom
when we lived next door.

Not much of a monument. But you
weren't much of a neighbor—
telling me to keep my dog
out of your yard, my daughter
away from your pyracanthas,
disturbing my sleep with your cries
until I fully waked, called the police
to break into your house,
help you out of your bathtub
where your defaulted, stubborn bones had collapsed.

We shared only a fierce need to survive.
You and your rock-hard face rocked on your porch
the day I moved in. No words
welcomed another fugitive
from a failed marriage.

But these blossoms

remind me of your fierceness;
what you taught me about hunkering down,
holding on to everything.
Especially what I stole from you.

Surviving Thanksgiving

When my father took me to visit his turkeys,
some photographer was waiting to catch us;
father in flannel shirt, me,
a little babushkad girl.

In the midst of a field of turkeys.
I had forgotten how his eyes opened space;
how blessed I felt when
we looked in on his birds

surrounded by turkey feathers, smell of their shit,
outrageous gurgling from deep catches in wattles,
straw and dust, beaks pecking my sleeves.

This scene, near killing time—most would get only one new moon
before losing their heads.

Their eyes, pins spinning into each other,
no love, no brains,
but they knew enough to peck each other
to death when it thundered.

I want that babushka,
his flannel shirt,
the smell of mash and turkey shit.
I want to go back to that moment
just before the turkeys were slaughtered.

At the State Theater

Saturday afternoons
Abbott keeps bashing
Costello or maybe
the other way
around who remembers
except for the pain

A fist to the breadbasket
chin to the skull, door
opening on nose, buckets
dropping on heads
Bashing
Ouching
Kapowing

A small child in the fifth row shouts
"Play nice," puts her hands
over her ears, sweater over her eyes,
wails as if the brick had dropped on her foot,
the match had started a fire in her hair

Why didn't she get the fighting was make-believe?
Perhaps early ambushes—
older brother jumping out of closets,
reenacting scenes from *Phantom of the Opera*

Or foreshadowing the life
to come—so much anger
would blur lines, leave her
forever wanting to make fantasy
real and reality make-believe.

A Broken Nose

Maybe she was attractive before
her brother slammed
on the brakes sending her nose
into the windshield in 1921
driving to Duluth.

The nose, profiled
in her wedding picture
1943 is long in the middle
where bone snapped pieces never
met—jagged ends
bumped like a full stop
or change in direction
nowhere to go but down
to the lip, whatever
it took to get there.

A series of breaks, all bad.
In the picture she's getting
her license to marry finally
sick of teaching school aging
in Racine each day
    during the six months
    they were married
    she brought him to visit
    I was six and he kissed
    me on the lips proving
    to my mother he was no good.

Under the second picture
she's asking $90 a month
he never gave her a dime
only the diamond
she added to other tokens
from broken engagements
to make a brooch.
"Bankrupt," the judge said.
"Give her $65 a month for six months."

Later, alone in Arizona
dying from cancer
she was brought back to her family,
the brooch went to me.

I sold her brooch after
crashing my car
through a guard rail
in the rain in 1978
breaking my nose
bone fragments met
even in profile
it looks almost straight.

She hadn't meant to die
without one second of joy.
My age when they buried her
and no one knows where
they buried the bastard
who promised the moon
and a fur coat and kissed
me on the lips like I was a piece
of fruit and he was the farmer.

Dancing at Bobby Zimmerman's Bar Mitzvah

What were they thinking
those children in 1954; he,
the blue-eyed son wrapped in
a wrinkled tallis, his yarmulke levitating
on that huge head of curls; the blue-eyed
girl tripping in new high heels,
back and shoulders bare
as an invitation.

Evening shone tender, blue
from inside, lighting up the town
as if the sun had refused to fully set.

The Androy Hotel, perched between
ore dumps and open pit mines, on Hibbing's
one main street, its Crystal Lounge
awash with his aunts, uncles—Irenes,
Sylvias, Labels, Mikeys—all congratulating,
guzzling champagne, wrapping their dreams
around the bar mitzvah boy,
all to the beat
of sambas and rumbas
imported from Duluth;
chandeliers reflecting
light in a hundred directions
rousing people who'd been hibernating
for years. His mother beamed
over her blue-eyed boy who'd go far—
medical or law school she predicted.
He looked dazed or
ashamed, kept his feet shuffling, fingers tapping,
eager to leave for somewhere else.

I, too, couldn't wait for those big-city lights,
attentive boys who knew how to dance, kiss.

No one would have guessed
how far we'd run after
the champagne was gone,
the guests coerced to their cars, homes,
and we had licenses of our own. But it was as far

from Hibbing—its open pit mines, its mounds
of red topsoil, winters of icy caves, and
summer nights sweet and fragrant as forget-me-nots—
as we could.

At 2 A.M., When Sleep Is Another Country

She weighs the color of night,
calibrates its density by what slips
through flapping curtains.

Listens for the plop of the newspaper
while the engine rolls away,
the neighbor's toilet flushing.

Nuzzles the sleeping shoulder
on the nearby pillow, despite sounds
of graveled snores, gives thanks
for this body ready to comfort,

recalls her parents' four-postered bed
from which they'd emerge
carrying warm milk and honey
if she could still cry and they were still alive.

Pictures babies waiting to be born,
covers her eyes with a black mask,
slips back into some night
where her name is written on fading stars.

The Importance of Having Something Rise When Everything Else Falls

That week she made bread,
sprinkled yeast onto warm water,
felt the smell of earth
seep into her flesh.

She measured in flour, waited
its rising, luxury of waiting.

Its dimensions doubled;
she kneaded the dough
using the heels of her hands
like cudgels, worked the sticky lump.
At first refusing
to form, it clung
to the board, to her hands.

She threw in flour, more flour,
fear flowed
from her shoulders,
arms, into her hands
until the sprawling mess turned
into a dense shape
to be twisted, glazed, baked.

Later, it emerged from the oven, warm,
redolent with proof that feelings
can transform, that there is something
a solitary woman can do
when there's nothing to do.

So Long Waiting

He hasn't seen me since I was a senior in high school. He'd point to his boyhood home two miles below the earth's surface on the floor of the open pit mine, color of dried blood laced by slender pockets of collected rain, machinery crawling like worms. He wouldn't recognize his daughter as grandmother. One day I will point to the speck on the map, general vicinity of my childhood home. A well-fed gull pecks at larvae hiding between its breast feathers. Backlit by the eerie glow of nocolor —seamless sky tucked between mountain ridges. Pangas, rowing shells, kayaks slither down the creek. They broke her water and the baby started its inevitable paddle downstream. He must be thinking, she was only seventeen. It was his stomach or liver long before Vietnam, before iron ore depleted itself. Egg of my egg, without chin, fingers too long for his hands. He'll learn about connections, first the easy way. Later it will be hard. Like the iron from ore, like a heart so long waiting.

Rowing in Fog

Oars into locks,
face to stern,
I head out, sensing
through blankets of fog
what I'm leaving behind.

Remembering what's hidden,
I imagine egrets and planes
silvering through sky,
mallards and sandpipers
nuzzling for worms,

know for certain only what reaches out—
mud scraped from bottom
(tide too low)
branches uprooted last winter by storms.

Down to the bridge,
turn, head back to the dock,
fog thinning, I see,
clearly now, where I've been.

Painting a Life

after Lisel Mueller

How I would paint hope

> An avocado pit pierced with a toothpick
> dangling in a translucent glass of water
> A princess phone, cream-colored
> An IV drip attached to the left hand

How I would paint fear

> Sky lightening toward dawn, moon slipping
> An IV drip attached to the left hand
> A princess phone, cream-colored

How I would paint desire

> An avocado pit pierced with a toothpick
> dangling in a translucent glass of water
> A white egret standing on one foot against a blue sky
> The smell of yeast starting to bubble

How I would paint regret

> A blank page, no lines, no marks, a slight gloss
> The vulnerable curve at the base of the throat
> Fingers on one hand numb with cold

How I would paint grief

> A blank page, no lines, no marks, a slight gloss
> Sheets stained with semen and blood
> Stratus clouds leaking into an autumn sky

How I would paint memory

       Sheets stained with semen and blood
       A gathering of pink begonias
       Dandelions fermenting in a ceramic crock

How I would paint joy

       I would not paint it. I would hire someone
       who trusted joy to put paint on paper, to cover
       the blank page, no lines no marks, a slight gloss.

WHAT
REMAINS

Shedding the Body

Next, a Japanese maple,
leaves unraveling
into steady air,
into cutouts of sky,
reversing foreground/background,
turning crimson and cold,
dropping all
pretence of proportion or insight.

Standing naked—all past
curling around its roots,
no looking down or up—
waiting
to make buds,
make leaves—and return.

Silent Cities

In 1966, we were killing
mothers and babies in Vietnam.
I wore a red jersey dress,
sleeveless. We drove
from dinner to marriage
as if it were dessert.

Predicted the day
we would walk backward
across the courtyard,
into the judge's office
say, "I don't"
and be undone.

Some things remain—
a child, photos, a name,

a book on the Mayas
Silent Cities
the buried cities—
Sayil, Kabah, Dzibichaltun—
buildings in ruin.

The jeep ride through heavy vines
to reach Labna before dark.

The driver's stories about snakes waiting
to grasp a woman's breasts,
suck out the milk.

Palenque—its white bones
rising from green jungle—
a skeleton picked
to a gleam.

We descended the tunnel
to the tomb of the prince,
his death mask radiant.

We crawled, that summer we married,
bellies in dust, breathing in bat shit
looking for clues, trying to learn
why they vanished.

In the Bridal Salon

I remember my elopement to Reno
after a night drinking in the red dress
I wore to work that day,
the judge unable to pronounce our names,

Overhear waiting mothers tell how they cried
seeing their daughters
in white. When my daughter
enters curtain right, I notice only her hands,
how uselessly they dangle,
tangled in *peau de soie* and lace
as she waits for me

to respond. But I'm seeing the wet, sour-smelling infant
who pulled herself up each morning,
stretched out her arms,
demanded "Up, up!"

How I'd grab her in my arms,
twirl her around the room,
for those moments, no sound
of my own despair, no sour taste
on my tongue.

I tell her it's beautiful but
it's not white veils
that will bring tears.
It's when she tells me, as she will,
that I've been the best of mothers.

Then the tears at the deception and the awe—
what we do when we think we're doing something
else, like surviving.

What You Do When There's Nothing to Do

After the daughter's lungs and kidneys fail
Call a manicurist to shape and polish her nails pale mauve

Buy her a hand-painted scarf in an abstract design
Commandeer a Jacuzzi, let her soak in gardenia-scented bubbles

Make listless tapioca—no matter
it's not her favorite, it was once yours

Wash your car so the hubcaps reflect the sun
Scrub your cupboards and line up the forks

Write a poem about death and salvation
Run down to the bay and back wearing fuchsia tights

Make reservations at the Soto Vento in Zihuatenejo, anticipate
coarse salt on your lips "when this is over"

Buy a book for the child she might not live to bear.

Flowing

Bay swells, unseasonably high, cover
encampments where geese gather
at lower tides to honk
at the sun or cavil
at each blackbird

while my daughter's fluids
also off track, run amuck;
kidneys, our amphibious relic,
confused, release what they should retain,
send fluid into the lungs
and spaces in between

At a signal, water changes direction,
courses eastward emptying the throughway,
joins the Sacramento runoff,
while she, puffed up, lies tethered to tubes
carrying fluids in and out
flushing and emptying
as if she were a tidal basin

We hold our breaths
hoping the absence of moisture
will steady her, put fluid
like those in the slough,
in the bay, into the veins,
draw it out of the lungs
keep it where it belongs

The geese are absent today,
their playground covered with debris;
air above their imprint holds
faint echoes of a screech I only now hear
as music, as an overarching call for help

This Will Break Your Heart

Like astronauts seeing what was meant only
for gods' eyes—earth's curve, sun's oscillation—
we felt awe

at the images of ancients touching.
Ramses, arm draped around
Nefertari's shoulder resting;
her arm curling across his sinewy back,
around his fleshy waist.
Tenderness ripens his satisfied lips;
her smile, honest and guarded,
sees through him into mystery.

Reminded of our own impermanence
we open, hold. And I, watching my companion,
this bulk of a man, mount a camel, his face wrapped
in fear and surprise, gather my feelings again
to place at his feet and hope
if someone should stumble
on the detritus of our lives
tomorrow, next year, four millennia from now,
they'll know
we cared for each other,
our arms gave comfort when we
were flesh and muscle.

Save the Inside Until Last

So now they're removing a tumor from your brain.
Last month, your wife,
the year before, your bladder, hip
and always the hair. Soon you'll be frame,
like those puzzles we put together
in the attic on Sixth Avenue.

Frame first, no looking at the picture (your rules).
     Each color its own pile,
all pieces turned over.

        Pictures of eighteenth-century English landscapes.
        From our attic window, snow to the edges.

No air in that room, just soft dust hovering.
Dad's trophies won by his famous dog,
Mom's wedding dress, *Time* magazines—one
from each week of the war,

our table under the pitch of roof
and oh, those pieces—the way the curves
linked into, hooked under each other.

Days went by, weeks.
You always placed the last piece
(held it back, pretended to find it).

We finished them all,
built a whole from pieces in that attic room
under the eaves where light lived
so sparingly.

I never looked when you destroyed
our finished puzzles.

Repetitive Motion

Surf unleashes,
gathers energy

Caught up in deep cycles of perpetual
patterns, rolls
toward the California coast
          reduces the infinite
to smash against
chaos to something controllable
                    erupting rocks sending (like dust or crumbs)
thick-whipped spray

collects everything palpable
into voluptuous clouds—

water slides into separate piles,
into shore, curls,
scoops itself up
again, around stone escarpments
          starts rolling,
settles into solace,

pushing,
drops plankton and salt

                              piling,
for anemones and urchins endless

                              emptying

More

Look at the old man fight
—as if the Cossacks were still
tracking him down, as if the class bullies
were still calling him kike.

Tethered to his bed
as if he might run away, join the circus,
a maze of tubes
without ending or beginning

he continues to force air
inout of his lungs
pulls at the catheter
urine spraying
like a Roman fountain.

Like a dancer, he curls his arms
around his head, arches his neck
angles his head onto his shoulder.

If he could see
he'd notice the buildings he put up
in his prime
when the ladies circled around

but today he's disappearing,
no more food—
forget the steaks, not even the pap
will dribble into his body.
Water and morphine they promise,
comforting angels of the dying.

If he could see himself, he'd give up the
ghost. He signed papers—
no tubes, no extraordinary measures, and still,
when push came to shove

he said More, maybe the way
we will all say More.

From Opposite Sides of the Glass

For Phyllis Diebenkorn

Hanging on my wall,
her face makes it easy
to marvel at his simplicity
of stroke, how he captures
a chin's power in three etched parabolic lines

makes her more
real than the face
in my mirror

But his triumph is her eyes,
they follow me, grab onto mine,
connect us in time and space;
we both sit wordless, enshrined
in our own kind of permanence
as if this moment were all

Her presence confirms how
all acts of creation erase
their creator,
reminds us
what remains is what remains.

Intention

Let me be the raucous hawking of Canadian geese huddled
around each other, keeping blackbirds away

> And the ear of the woman aging despite her intentions,
> which hears their dangerous speech

The water flowing back to the bay dappled with sunspecks,
stripes of harmonic ripples

> And the eye of the woman aging despite her intentions,
> which sees the steady beat of the tide

The breeze begging leaves on the willow,
hairs on the arms to follow it downstream

> And the skin of the woman aging despite her intentions,
> which feels the cloud's moist breath

The succulent look of the lover aroused,
fingers and lips searching and finding

> And the flesh of the woman aging despite her intentions,
> which begs to be sucked dry

The late autumn sun dividing its rays, softly cooking
what it claims for its own

> And the naked body of the woman aging despite her intentions,
> which turns hot inside and out

Let me be the laughter of the dead parents, echoing abundantly
decades after their deaths

> And the will of the woman aging
> who pulls the dead back to life, holds them as long as she can.

NOTES

The epigraph for "What I Stole" is from *Einstein's Dreams*, by Alan Lightman (Random House), reprinted with permission from the publisher.

The words on the retablo described in "Donaciana Aquiree Gives Thanks" were written by an unnamed painter or by Donaciana Aquiree herself.

The italicized phrases from "Painting a Life" are from "Imaginary Paintings" by Lisel Mueller.

Diane Sher Lutovich, a writer and teacher of writing, is a native of Hibbing, Minnesota (along with Bob Dylan). She now lives near an outlet of the Pacific in the San Francisco Bay Area. Her poetry has received several awards, including those from The Lake Superior Writers Council and the Council on Aging, and her work has appeared in numerous literary reviews and anthologies. She is the author of *Nobody's Child: How Older Women Say Good-bye to Their Mothers*, published by Baywood Press.

The text font used for *What I Stole* is Photina, designed by José Mendoza y Almeida and commissioned by Monotype in 1972. The display font on the cover and section openers is called Rusticana. Both fonts carry an unmistakable calligraphic energy.

Sixteen Rivers Press is a shared-work, not-for-profit poetry collective dedicated to providing an alternative publishing avenue for San Francisco Bay Area poets. Founded in 1999 by seven women writers, the press is named for the sixteen rivers that flow into San Francisco Bay.

16 RIVERS
P R E S S

SAN JOAQUIN ◆ FRESNO ◆ CHOWCHILLA ◆ MERCED ◆ TUOLUMNE
STANISLAUS ◆ CALAVERAS ◆ BEAR ◆ MOKELUMNE ◆ COSUMNES
AMERICAN ◆ YUBA ◆ FEATHER ◆ SACRAMENTO ◆ NAPA ◆ PETALUMA

Also from Sixteen Rivers Press

difficult news by Valerie Berry
Translations from the Human Language by Terry Ehret
After Cocteau by Carolyn Miller
Snake at the Wrist by Margaret Kaufman
Sacred Precinct by Jacqueline Kudler